I A

D1144608

Let's Explore

Babies

by Henry Pluckrose

W

FRANKLIN WATTS

NEW YORK • LONDON • SYDNEY

Author's note

This book is one of a series which has been designed to encourage young readers to think about the everyday concepts that form part of their world. The text and photographs complement each other, and both elements combine to provide starting points for discussion. Although each book is complete in itself, each title links closely with others in the set, so presenting an ideal platform for learning.

I have consciously avoided 'writing down' to my readers. Young children like to know the 'real' words for things, and are better able to express themselves when they can use correct terms with confidence.

Young children learn from the experiences they share with adults around them. The child offers his or her ideas which are then developed and extended through the adult. The books in this series are a means for the child and adult to share informal talk, photographs and text, and the ideas which accompany them.

One particular element merits comment. Information books are also reading books. Like a successful story book, an effective information book will be turned to again and again. As children develop, their appreciation of the significance of fact develops too. The young child who asks 'Where did I come from, Mummy?' may subsequently and more provocatively ask, 'How did Daddy help you make me?' Thoughts take time to generate. Hopefully books like those in this series provide the momentum for this.

Henry Pluckrose

Contents

Every moment of every day,
every moment of every night,
somewhere in the world,
a baby is being born.

Before babies are born, they live and grow inside the mother's body for about 280 days. The mother's tummy. grows bigger: the baby needs room to grow.

New-born babies are just like you.
They have eyes, ears, a mouth,
a nose, tiny fingers and toes,
and sometimes even hair.

The surprise of being born
makes the baby cry.
The baby takes oxygen
from the air and begins to breathe.

A baby needs food and warmth, sleep and love, just like you do.

A new-born baby can
only swallow liquid food.
Milk from the mother is best.
Sometimes, babies are fed
with special milk from bottles.

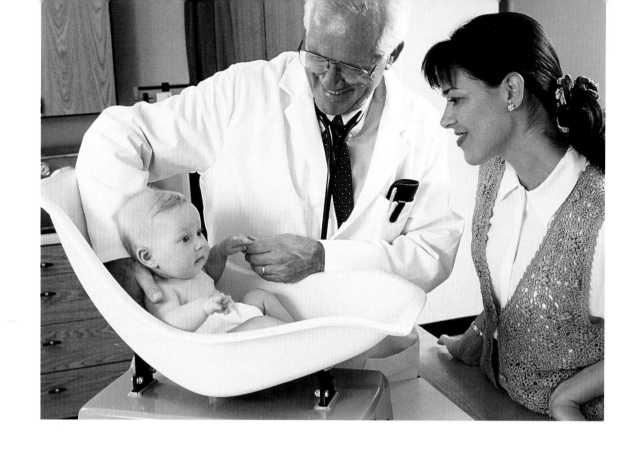

After babies are born,
they are weighed and measured.
How heavy were you
when you were born?

In poor countries, some babies
are too small and weak to live.

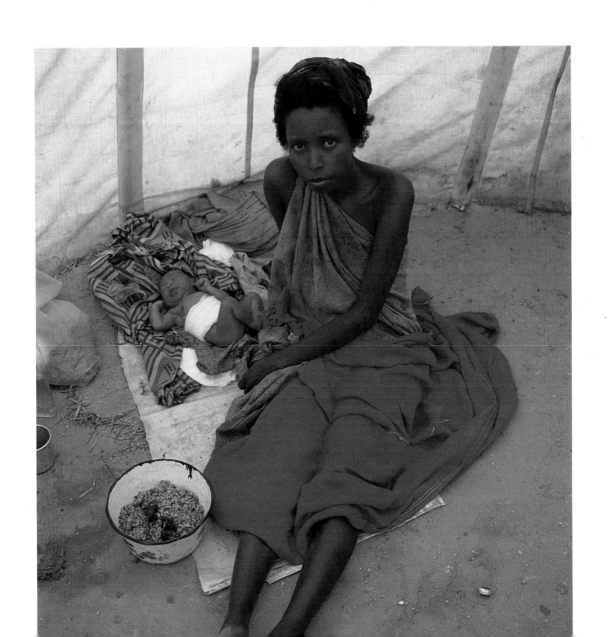

In rich countries,
there are hospitals
to care for sick babies.
An incubator is a special cot
to keep babies warm,
and to help them breathe.

Sometimes, two babies grow
inside the mother's tummy
at the same time.
These babies are called twins.
Twins can look exactly the same,
or they can look quite different.

When you were small,
you could not speak.
You smiled when you were happy.
You cried when you were not.

23

Like all babies, you grew.

You began to make sounds.

You began to crawl.

You stood up and began to walk.

You copied the sounds
you heard around you.
Your baby babble became words.
Babies from different countries
make different word sounds.

Animals have babies too.

Kittens grow inside the mother cat.

Kittens need food,

warmth and care,

just like human babies.

Human babies take many years
to grow into men and women.
When you have children,
do you think your mother
will like being called 'Granny'?

Index

First published in 1999 by
Franklin Watts
96 Leonard Street
London
EC2A 4XD

Franklin Watts Australia
14 Mars Road
Lane Cove
NSW 2066

Copyright © Franklin Watts 1999

ISBN 0 7496 3464 2

Dewey Decimal
Classification Number 649

A CIP catalogue record for this book is
available from the British Library

Series editor: Louise John
Series designer: Jason Anscomb

Printed in Hong Kong

Picture Credits:
Steve Shott Photography pp. 4, 12, 14, 15, 22,
23, 24, 25, 27, cover and title page; Bubbles
pp. 8 (Jennie Woodcock), 11 (Clarissa
Leahy), 19 (Frans Rombout), 20 (Moose
Azim); The Image Bank pp. 7 (HMS
Images), 16 (Janeart), 31 (Nancy Brown);
Robert Harding p. 17 (A. D Projects); Bruce
Coleman p. 28 (Hans Reinhard).